Oceans and Seas

Southern Ocean

Kate A. Furlong
ABDO Publishing Company

visit us at
www.abdopub.com

Published by ABDO Publishing Company, 4940 Viking Drive, Edina, Minnesota 55435.
Copyright © 2003 by Abdo Consulting Group, Inc. International copyrights reserved in
all countries. No part of this book may be reproduced in any form without written
permission from the publisher.

Printed in the United States.

Photo Credits: Corbis

Contributing Editors: Kristin Van Cleaf, Kristianne E. Vieregger
Art Direction & Graphics: Neil Klinepier

Library of Congress Cataloging-in-Publication Data

Furlong, Kate A., 1977-
    Southern Ocean / Kate A. Furlong.
        p. cm. -- (Oceans and seas)
    Includes index.
    Summary: Provides information about the newly delineated ocean that surrounds the
continent of Antarctica.
    ISBN 1-57765-991-0
    1. Antarctic Ocean--Juvenile literature. [1. Antarctic Ocean.] I. Title. II. Series.

GC461 .F87 2003
551.46'9--dc21

                                                                          2002028328

Contents

The Southern Ocean 4

Forming the Floor 6

Southern Water 8

Climate 10

Plants 12

Animals 14

Explorers Arrive 16

Interest Continues 18

Today's Southern Ocean 20

Glossary 22

How Do You Say That? 23

Web Sites 23

Index 24

The Southern Ocean

The Southern Ocean has fascinated explorers and scientists for centuries. Its cold, rough waters completely surround the continent of Antarctica. For this reason, the Southern Ocean is sometimes called the Antarctic Ocean.

The Southern Ocean has not always been considered a separate ocean. However, in 2000 the **International Hydrographic Organization** officially established the Southern Ocean's boundaries. They extend from Antarctica to 60° south **latitude**.

Today, the Southern Ocean is the fourth-largest ocean in the world. It includes many smaller bodies of water. For example, the Amundsen **Sea**, Bellingshausen Sea, Weddell Sea, and Ross Sea are all parts of the Southern Ocean.

4

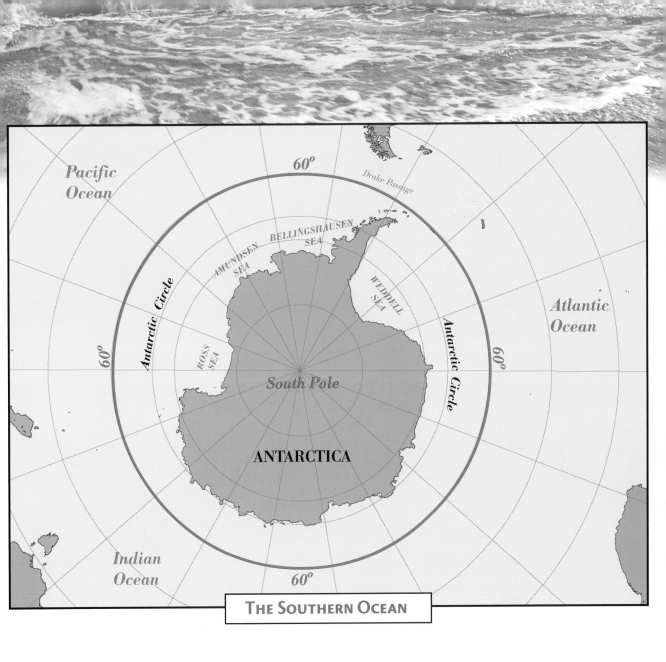

Pacific
Ocean

60°

Drake Passage

BELLINGSHAUSEN
SEA

AMUNDSEN
SEA

Antarctic Circle

60°

ROSS
SEA

WEDDELL
SEA

Antarctic Circle

60°

Atlantic
Ocean

South Pole

ANTARCTICA

Indian
Ocean

60°

THE SOUTHERN OCEAN

Forming the Floor

Millions of years ago, Earth had only one continent. It was called Pangaea. It was surrounded by Earth's only ocean, Panthalassa. About 200 million years ago, Pangaea began to break into pieces. One of the large pieces was called Gondwana.

Eventually, Gondwana began breaking into pieces, too. These pieces became Antarctica, South America, and Africa. During this time, the Weddell **Sea** formed. It is the oldest part of the Southern Ocean.

Moving clockwise from the Weddell Sea, the ocean floor gets younger. This is because India, Australia, and New Zealand later broke from Antarctica in a clockwise pattern. As each piece broke off, new ocean floor formed.

Today, the pieces that broke from Gondwana are still moving away from Antarctica. As this happens, new ocean floor forms. The ocean floor expands about one-half to four inches (14 to 100 mm) each year.

For many years, scientists thought the Southern Ocean's floor was a giant trench. They imagined it looked like a **moat** circling Antarctica. But recently, scientists have discovered that it has a system of basins, plains, ridges, channels, and canyons.

THE SOUTHERN OCEAN FLOOR

Bellingshausen Plain

Weddell Plain

Pacific-Antarctic Ridge

Enderby Plain

Atlantic-Indian Ridge

South Indian Basin

Southern Water

Water in the Southern Ocean is cold. **Ice shelves** extend from Antarctica's coast. Every year, thousands of ice pieces break off the ice shelves, forming icebergs. The Southern Ocean may have up to 300,000 icebergs at any given time.

The ice along Antarctica's coast cools the Southern Ocean's water. The cool water sinks to the ocean bottom. Then the water flows north. Eventually, it meets the warmer waters of the Atlantic, Pacific, and Indian Oceans.

Some icebergs in the Southern Ocean are a mile (1.6 km) long.

The warm and cold waters meet at an area called the Antarctic Convergence. There, the warmer water rises, flows south, and forms the Southern Ocean's surface water. This warm water is the main source of heat in the Southern Ocean.

The Southern Ocean also contains the world's largest **current**. The Antarctic Circumpolar Current flows from west to east around Antarctica. It is the only current that can travel around the world without being blocked by a continent.

Small icebergs are often called growlers. Larger icebergs are often called bergy bits.

Climate

The Southern Ocean is in the Southern **Hemisphere**. The seasons there are opposite to the seasons in the Northern Hemisphere. That means in Antarctica, summer is in December, and winter is in June.

In the winter, more than half of the Southern Ocean's surface water freezes. In the summer, most of this ice melts. These changes in the ocean's ice cover have a major effect on winds.

The Southern Ocean has some of the strongest winds on Earth. Winds near the coast can reach 180 miles per hour (290 km/h). Strong, cold winds and rough water are especially common at Drake Passage. This waterway is located between Antarctica and South America.

Opposite page: Ice covering the Southern Ocean

Plants

Plants that grow in Antarctica and the Southern Ocean are hardy. They must be able to survive the Antarctic's harsh winters. Winters have freezing temperatures and little sunlight.

About 400 kinds of phytoplankton grow in the Southern Ocean. These tiny plants bloom in the spring and summer when there is plenty of sunlight. They are a major part of the Southern Ocean's **food chain**.

Algae also live in the Southern Ocean. In the winter, these plants are trapped in the ocean's ice. In the spring, they begin to grow again. As the ice slowly melts, algae return to the water. There, they are a major food source for small animals.

A large type of algae called kelp lives in the Southern Ocean, too. Kelp forests grow in the shallow water near islands. During storms, they protect the shores of the islands. The kelp forests also support many kinds of fish and birds.

Lichens are plants that are hardy enough to survive in the Antarctic region. These lichens are growing on an island in the Southern Ocean.

Animals

Many animals live in the Southern Ocean. Krill are shrimp-like animals. They live in large groups near the Antarctic Convergence. Whales, fish, birds, and seals all rely on krill as a food source. This makes krill an important part of the **food chain**.

Several kinds of whales live in the Southern Ocean. The blue whale is Earth's largest animal. In the summer, blue whales live in the Southern Ocean near Antarctica's **ice shelves**. In the winter, they swim to warmer waters to **breed**.

A fur seal

Seals also live in the Southern Ocean. Antarctic fur seals have gray, brown, or silver coats. In the

Penguins dive into the Southern Ocean.

1800s, hunters killed many of these seals for their coats. Today, the Antarctic Treaty protects fur seals.

The Southern Ocean is also home to several kinds of penguins. Though they cannot fly, these birds are excellent swimmers. Penguins build their nests on land. They travel to the ocean to find food.

More than 270 fish species live in the Southern Ocean. Many of them have adapted to the ocean's cold water. For example, the icefish's blood contains a type of **antifreeze**. It allows an icefish to survive in water cold enough to kill other fish.

Explorers Arrive

No **indigenous** people have ever lived in Antarctica. For centuries, the Southern Ocean's rough water stopped people from finding the continent.

In the 1770s, English explorer James Cook searched for Antarctica. Cook sailed through fog, snow, and rough water. In 1773, Cook became the first person to cross the **Antarctic Circle**. Yet, he did not find Antarctica.

James Cook

In Cook's notes, he mentioned that many seals and whales lived in the Antarctic region. Soon, hunters in search of profits traveled to the Southern Ocean. They discovered nearly a third of the ocean's islands. However, they never found Antarctica.

Explorers finally discovered Antarctica in 1820. That year, American Nathaniel Palmer, Englishman Edward Bransfield, and Russian Fabian Gottlieb von Bellingshausen each claimed to see Antarctica first.

James Cook and his crew battle icebergs.

Interest Continues

Robert F. Scott

After the discovery of Antarctica, interest in the continent continued to grow. Englishmen Robert F. Scott and Ernest Henry Shackleton braved the rough Southern Ocean to reach Antarctica. During the early 1900s, they studied the continent and made routes to its interior.

Soon, many explorers began trying to reach the South Pole. Explorer Roald Amundsen of Norway used **sledges** pulled by dogs to travel across Antarctica. In 1911, Amundsen became the first person to reach the South Pole.

Ernest Henry Shackleton

18

Shackleton's base camp on the Ross Ice Shelf

Between 1908 and 1942, seven nations claimed to rule parts of Antarctica. This led to the Antarctic Treaty, which 12 nations signed in 1959. It preserved the continent for scientific research. It forbade building military bases, testing weapons, or disposing waste in Antarctica.

Today's Southern Ocean

The Antarctic region continues to fascinate scientists. Several nations have set up research stations in Antarctica and on islands in the Southern Ocean. The scientists study the region's plants, animals, land, ice, and climate.

Scientists have many ways to study the Southern Ocean itself. **Satellites** collect images of the ocean. Underwater vehicles can travel more than 1,000 feet (305 m) under the **ice shelves**. They can also gather information about the ocean's deepest, coldest water.

Today, the Antarctic Treaty continues to preserve the region for the future. It allows for Specially Protected Areas (SPAs) and Sites of Special Scientific Interest (SSSIs). SPAs and SSSIs protect parts of the region from tourists and other unofficial visitors.

The Antarctic Treaty protects the Southern Ocean's cold, icy coast for the future.

Glossary

Antarctic Circle - an imaginary line in the Southern Hemisphere that runs parallel to the equator at about 66° south latitude.

antifreeze - a substance that prevents liquids from freezing in cold temperatures.

breed - to produce offspring.

current - a stream of water that flows through a larger body of water, such as an ocean.

food chain - an arrangement of plants and animals in a community. Each plant or animal feeds on other plants or animals in a certain order. For example, phytoplankton are eaten by small fish, small fish are eaten by large fish, and large fish are eaten by humans.

hemisphere - one-half of Earth.

ice shelf - an ice sheet that begins on land and extends into the ocean.

indigenous - native.

International Hydrographic Organization - an international organization established in 1921. It works to protect and study Earth's oceans.

latitude - the distance north or south from the equator. Latitude is measured in degrees.

moat - a deep trench that is usually filled with water.

satellite - a human-made object that orbits Earth.

sea - a body of water that is smaller than an ocean and is almost completely surrounded by land.

sledge - a strong sled.

How Do You Say That?

algae - AL-jee
circumpolar - suhr-kihm-POH-luhr
convergence - kuhn-VUHR-juhnts
Gondwana - gawn-DWAH-nuh
hemisphere - HEH-muh-sfihr
indigenous - in-DIH-juh-nuhs
Pangaea - pan-JEE-uh
Panthalassa - pan-THA-luh-suh
phytoplankton - fi-toh-PLANGK-tuhn

Web Sites

Would you like to learn more about the Southern Ocean? Please visit **www.abdopub.com** to find up-to-date Web site links about the Southern Ocean, its creatures, and its harsh environment. These links are routinely monitored and updated to provide the most current information available.

Index

A

Africa 6
Amundsen, Roald 18
Amundsen Sea 4
animals 12, 14, 15, 16, 20
Antarctic Circle 16
Antarctic Circumpolar Current 9
Antarctic Convergence 9, 14
Antarctic Treaty 15, 19, 20
Antarctica 4, 6, 7, 8, 9, 10, 12, 14, 16, 17, 18, 19, 20
Atlantic Ocean 8
Australia 6

B

Bellingshausen, Fabian Gottlieb von 17
Bellingshausen Sea 4
Bransfield, Edward 17

C

climate 10, 12, 20
Cook, James 16

D

Drake Passage 10

E

exploration 4, 16, 17, 18

G

Gondwana 6

I

ice shelves 8, 14, 20
icebergs 8
India 6
Indian Ocean 8
International Hydrographic Organization 4
islands 12, 17, 20

N

New Zealand 6
Norway 18

O

ocean floor 6, 7, 8

P

Pacific Ocean 8
Palmer, Nathaniel 17
Pangaea 6
Panthalassa 6
plants 12, 20

R

Ross Sea 4

S

scientific research 4, 7, 19, 20
Scott, Robert F. 18
seasons 10, 12, 14
Shackleton, Ernest Henry 18
South America 6, 10
South Pole 18

W

Weddell Sea 4, 6